BUILDING WEALTH
with
CRYPTO

Unlock the secrets of cryptocurrency and embrace the future of finance. Your guide to invest in cryptocurrencies and take control of your financial destiny with confidence and clarity.

MARCEL ISLER

First Edition: March 2024

ISBN 978-3-9526019-1-4   US $ 12.90

Welcome to "Building Wealth with Crypto: Unlock the secrets of cryptocurrency and embrace the future of finance." a comprehensive guide crafted for those intrigued by the burgeoning world of cryptocurrency yet unsure where to begin. This book is a beacon for beginners, offering a clear path through the often complex and misunderstood landscape of digital currencies.

The genesis of this guide was inspired by a simple observation: despite the growing prominence of cryptocurrencies in the global financial landscape, a vast majority of potential investors remain on the sidelines, overwhelmed by the technology's perceived complexity and the market's volatility. Our aim is to bridge this gap, providing a structured and understandable introduction to cryptocurrency, its potential for wealth creation, and the strategies for successful investment.

This book is structured to cater to readers with varying levels of understanding and experience. Starting with the fundamentals, we delve into the origins and unique characteristics of cryptocurrencies, offering a solid foundation upon which to build your knowledge. From there, we navigate through the practical aspects of getting started in the crypto market, including choosing the right wallets and exchanges, understanding market dynamics, and developing effective investment strategies.

As your confidence grows, we introduce more advanced topics such as risk management, staking, yield farming, leveraging, and margin trading. These concepts are presented with clarity and caution, emphasizing the importance of informed decision-making and risk mitigation.

Beyond the mechanics of trading and investment, this guide explores the broader implications and applications of blockchain technology. We delve into its transformative potential across various industries, the evolving regulatory landscape, and the critical role of security and community within the crypto space.

Our journey concludes with a forward-looking discussion on integrating cryptocurrency into your overall financial plan and a glimpse into the future of cryptocurrency investing. Here, we speculate on emerging trends, technological advancements, and the global trajectory of digital currencies.

This book is not merely a guide to cryptocurrency investment; it is an invitation to join a revolutionary movement reshaping our financial systems and societal structures. It's about empowering you with the knowledge and tools to take control of your financial future in this new digital frontier.

Thank you for choosing this guide as your entry point into the world of cryptocurrency. May it light your path toward informed investment decisions, financial growth, and participation in the economic systems of tomorrow.

Welcome to the journey. Let's embark on this adventure together.

This book, "Building Wealth with Crypto: Unlock the secrets of cryptocurrency and embrace the future of finance." is designed for a wide audience with varying levels of familiarity with cryptocurrency, specifically catering to:

1. **Absolute Beginners**: Individuals who have heard about cryptocurrency but have little to no understanding of what it is, how it works, or how to get started with investing in it. This book aims to demystify the world of cryptocurrencies, providing a solid foundation for newcomers.

2. **Aspiring Investors**: Those who are interested in diversifying their investment portfolio by including cryptocurrencies but are unsure of the strategies, risks, and potential rewards. The book offers insights into various investment approaches, including long-term holding and short-term trading, along with advanced investment techniques.

3. **Tech Enthusiasts**: Individuals fascinated by blockchain technology and its applications beyond cryptocurrencies, such as NFTs and decentralized finance (DeFi). This book delves into how blockchain is transforming various industries and the implications for future technological developments.

4. **Financial Planners**: People looking to understand how cryptocurrencies fit into broader financial planning, including retirement and estate planning. The book provides guidance on integrating digital currencies into an overall financial strategy.

5. **Risk-Averse Individuals**: Those who are cautious about the volatile nature of the cryptocurrency market but are curious about exploring this space. The book covers essential risk management strategies, legal and tax implications, and how to protect investments.

6. **Community Seekers**: Individuals interested in the cultural and communal aspects of cryptocurrency investing, including leveraging social media, forums, and networking opportunities within the crypto community. The book highlights the importance of community support and collaboration in the crypto ecosystem.

7. **Future-Focused Readers**: Those curious about the future of cryptocurrency and emerging trends, including the impact of AI and quantum computing on the crypto market. The book offers predictions and discusses the global adoption of cryptocurrencies.

By covering a comprehensive range of topics, from foundational knowledge to advanced investment strategies and the future of cryptocurrency, this book serves as a valuable resource for anyone looking to understand or deepen their knowledge of cryptocurrency and its potential to impact financial planning and investment strategies.

WHAT THIS BOOK COVERS

Feedback from our readers is always welcome.

General feedback: If you have questions about any aspect of this book, mention the book title in the subject of your message and email us at hello@imiblockchain.com.

Errata: Although we have taken every care to ensure the accuracy of our content, mistakes do happen. If you have found a mistake in this book, we would be grateful if you would report this to us. Please message and email us at hello@imiblockchain.com.

Piracy: If you come across any illegal copies of our works in any form on the internet, we would be grateful if you would provide us with the location address or website name. Please contact us at hello@imiblockchain.com with a link to the material.

REVIEWS

Please leave a review. Once you have read and used this book, why not leave a review on the site that you purchased it from? Potential readers can then see and use your unbiased opinion to make purchase decisions, we at iMi Blockchain can understand what you think about our products, and our author can see your feedback on their book. Thank you!

For more information about iMi Blockchain, please visit **imiblockchain.com**

INTRODUCTION TO CRYPTOCURRENCY

Welcome to the fascinating world of cryptocurrency! Whether you've heard about Bitcoin on the news or are curious about how digital currencies work, this guide is designed to introduce you to the basics of cryptocurrency. We'll explore its history, what makes it unique, the different types available, and how it all works. Let's dive in!

CHAPTER 1

UNDERSTANDING CRYPTOCURRENCY

History of Cryptocurrency

The journey of cryptocurrency began in 2008 with the publication of a paper by an individual or group using the pseudonym Satoshi Nakamoto. This paper introduced Bitcoin and the concept of a decentralized digital currency. The idea was to create a system where transactions could be made directly between two parties without the need for a central authority, such as a bank or government. Bitcoin became the first cryptocurrency when it was released as open-source software in 2009.

Over the years, thousands of cryptocurrencies have been developed, each with its own unique features and purposes. The creation of Ethereum in 2015 marked another significant milestone, introducing smart contracts and paving the way for a new world of decentralized applications (dApps).

What Makes Cryptocurrency Unique

Cryptocurrencies are unique for several reasons:

- **Decentralization**: Unlike traditional currencies controlled by governments, cryptocurrencies operate on a decentralized network of computers. This makes them less susceptible to control or manipulation by any single entity.
- **Blockchain Technology**: Cryptocurrencies use blockchain technology to maintain a secure and transparent record of transactions. This technology ensures that all transactions are immutable, meaning they cannot be altered or deleted.
- **Anonymity and Privacy**: While transactions are transparent and recorded on the blockchain, the identities of the parties involved are encrypted. This offers a level of privacy and security for users.
- **Global Accessibility**: Cryptocurrencies can be sent or received anywhere in the world, provided there's an internet connection. This makes them accessible to people without access to traditional banking systems.

Types of Cryptocurrencies

- **Bitcoin (BTC)**: The first and most well-known cryptocurrency, often referred to as digital gold.
- **Ethereum (ETH)**: Known for its smart contract functionality, which allows for the creation of decentralized applications.
- **Altcoins**: A term for cryptocurrencies other than Bitcoin. Examples include Litecoin (LTC), Ripple (XRP), and many

others. Altcoins often aim to improve upon Bitcoin's technology or offer different features.

- **Tokens**: Unlike cryptocurrencies that operate on their own blockchain, tokens are built on existing blockchains. They can represent assets or be used within specific ecosystems. Examples include ERC-20 tokens on the Ethereum network.

How Cryptocurrencies Work

Cryptocurrencies operate on a technology called blockchain, a distributed ledger that records all transactions across a network of computers. Here's a simplified explanation:

- **Blockchain**: Imagine a chain where each link is a block containing transaction data. Each new block is connected to the previous one, creating a secure and unalterable chain of transactions.
- **Mining**: This is the process by which transactions are verified and added to the blockchain. Miners use powerful computers to solve complex mathematical problems. The first to solve the problem gets to add a new block to the blockchain and is rewarded with cryptocurrency.
- **Wallets**: To use cryptocurrency, you need a digital wallet. Wallets can be software (online, desktop, or mobile) or hardware-based. They store the cryptographic keys necessary to send and receive cryptocurrency.

This introduction has laid the foundation for your journey into the world of cryptocurrency. By understanding its history, what makes it unique, the various types available, and how it operates, you're well on your way to exploring the potential of digital currencies. Remember, the field of cryptocurrency is vast and constantly evolving, so continuous learning is key to staying informed.

CHAPTER 2

THE FINANCIAL POTENTIAL OF CRYPTOCURRENCY

In this chapter, we will explore the financial potential of cryptocurrency, providing you with a balanced view by examining both success stories and notable failures. Understanding the inherent volatility of the crypto market, its growth trends, and how it compares to traditional investments will empower you to make informed decisions as you navigate your investment journey.

Case Studies of Success and Failure

Success Stories

Bitcoin Early Adopters: One of the most well-known success stories is that of early Bitcoin adopters. Individuals who invested in Bitcoin during its infancy (2009-2012) saw astronomical returns as its value soared from a few cents to tens of thousands of dollars per coin. For example, someone who invested $100 in Bitcoin in 2010, when the price was around $0.08, would have owned 1,250 bitcoins. If they held onto those coins, their investment would have peaked at over $60 million during Bitcoin's all-time high in 2021.

Ethereum and ICO Boom: Another success story comes from the rise of Ethereum and the initial coin offering (ICO) craze of 2017. Ethereum's platform enabled startups to issue their own tokens to raise funds. Early investors in successful projects like Binance Coin (BNB) or Chainlink (LINK) saw significant returns on their investments as these projects flourished.

Notable Failures

The Mt. Gox Meltdown: In 2014, Mt. Gox, one of the largest Bitcoin exchanges at the time, filed for bankruptcy after losing 850,000 bitcoins due to hacking. This event crashed the Bitcoin market and left many investors with substantial losses, highlighting the risks of exchange failures.

The ICO Bubble and Scams: The ICO boom of 2017 also saw its fair share of failures and scams. Many projects that raised millions of dollars failed to deliver on their promises or were outright scams, leading to significant losses for investors. This period serves as a cautionary tale about the importance of due diligence.

Market Volatility and Growth Trends

Cryptocurrency markets are known for their high volatility, with prices capable of making substantial moves in a short period. Several factors contribute to this volatility:

- **Market Sentiment**: News, social media, and developments within the crypto space can rapidly affect market sentiment, leading to swift price movements.
- **Regulation News**: Announcements of new regulations or governmental positions on cryptocurrency can have immediate impacts on prices.
- **Technological Developments**: Innovations or issues within a blockchain project can influence investor confidence and, consequently, the price.

Despite the volatility, the cryptocurrency market has shown significant growth trends over the past decade. The total market capitalization of cryptocurrencies has expanded from less than $1 billion in 2013 to over $2 trillion at its peak. This growth is not only due to the increasing value of cryptocurrencies like Bitcoin and Ethereum but also the proliferation of new cryptocurrencies and blockchain projects.

Cryptocurrency vs Traditional Investments

When comparing cryptocurrency to traditional investments like stocks, bonds, and real estate, several differences become apparent:

- **Higher Volatility**: As mentioned, cryptocurrencies exhibit higher volatility than most traditional investments, offering the potential for higher returns but also greater risk.

- **Market Hours**: Unlike traditional markets, which have set trading hours, cryptocurrency markets operate 24/7, leading to continuous price changes.
- **Entry Barrier**: Cryptocurrencies have a lower entry barrier compared to some traditional investments, allowing individuals to start investing with small amounts.
- **Regulation and Security**: The regulatory environment for cryptocurrencies is less developed than for traditional financial markets, posing additional risks and uncertainties.

Investing in cryptocurrency presents a unique set of opportunities and challenges. While there are stories of remarkable gains, the risks are equally significant. Understanding these dynamics is crucial for anyone looking to explore the financial potential of cryptocurrency. As with any investment, thorough research, a clear strategy, and an awareness of your risk tolerance are key to navigating the crypto market successfully.

PART I
GETTING STARTED WITH CRYPTOCURRENCY

Embarking on your cryptocurrency investment journey can be both exciting and daunting. This section is designed to guide absolute beginners through the initial steps of getting involved in the crypto market, covering essential tools and resources, understanding market dynamics, and outlining fundamental investment strategies. By the end of this section, you will be well-equipped to start your investment journey with confidence.

CHAPTER 3

SETTING UP FOR SUCCESS

Essential Tools and Resources

Cryptocurrency Wallets: A digital wallet is your first necessity for holding and transacting in cryptocurrencies. Wallets come in various forms, including software (desktop and mobile), online (web), and hardware (physical devices). While software and online wallets offer convenience, hardware wallets provide enhanced security by storing your cryptocurrencies offline.

Exchanges: To buy, sell, or trade cryptocurrencies, you will need to use a cryptocurrency exchange. There are centralized exchanges (CEXs) like Coinbase and Binance, which act as intermediaries, and decentralized exchanges (DEXs) like Uniswap, which allow peer-to-peer transactions without a central authority.

News Sources: Staying informed is crucial in the fast-paced world of cryptocurrency. Follow reputable news outlets, forums like Reddit's r/cryptocurrency, and social media platforms for the latest updates, trends, and analyses.

Understanding the Market

Market Cap: The market capitalization of a cryptocurrency is a key metric for assessing its market size, calculated by multiplying the current price by the total number of coins in circulation. A higher market cap often indicates a more established and widely adopted cryptocurrency.

Volume: Trading volume shows the amount of a cryptocurrency traded within a specific period. High volume indicates high interest and liquidity, which can lead to more stable prices.

Price Changes: Cryptocurrency prices are highly volatile. Understanding the factors that influence price changes, such as market sentiment, news events, and overall market trends, can help in making informed investment decisions.

Legal and Tax Implications

Cryptocurrency regulations vary by country and can affect how you invest, store, and use your digital assets. It's important to be aware of your local laws regarding cryptocurrency taxation, reporting requirements, and what constitutes legal usage.

CHAPTER 4

INVESTMENT STRATEGIES

Long-term Holding vs Short-term Trading

Long-term Holding (HODLing): Many investors choose to hold cryptocurrencies for the long term, based on the belief that their value will increase over time. This strategy requires patience and a tolerance for market volatility.

Short-term Trading: This involves buying and selling cryptocurrencies over shorter periods to profit from price fluctuations. While it can offer quick returns, it requires a good understanding of the market and carries higher risk.

Diversification Strategies in Crypto

Diversification involves spreading your investment across multiple cryptocurrencies to reduce risk. Consider diversifying not only across different coins but also across different

categories (e.g., currencies, platforms, utilities) and investment types (e.g., staking, yield farming).

Identifying and Investing in ICOs and Tokens

Initial Coin Offerings (ICOs) and token sales can offer early
investment opportunities in new projects. Researching the
project's team, vision, technology, and community support is
crucial before investing.

CHAPTER 5

TECHNICAL ANALYSIS AND MARKET TRENDS

Reading Charts and Patterns

Understanding charts and patterns is fundamental for predicting future market movements. Learn to read candlestick charts, which show price movements over time, and recognize patterns that indicate potential price changes.

Key Indicators and Metrics

Relative Strength Index (RSI): Measures whether a cryptocurrency is overbought or oversold, providing signals for potential reversals.

Moving Average Convergence Divergence (MACD): Indicates the momentum of price movements, helping to identify trend reversals.

Volume: As mentioned, high trading volume can validate price movements, making it an important metric for traders.

The Impact of News and Events on Prices

News and events can have immediate effects on cryptocurrency prices. Developments such as regulatory changes, technological advancements, or significant partnerships can drive market sentiment and price movements. Staying informed and learning to anticipate the market's reaction to news is crucial for successful investing.

By familiarizing yourself with the tools, understanding market dynamics, adopting a sound investment strategy, and learning to analyze market trends, you'll be well on your way to becoming a successful crypto investor. Remember, the key to success in the cryptocurrency market is continuous learning and adapting to its ever-changing nature.

PART II
ADVANCED INVESTMENT TECHNIQUES

This section is tailored for those who have grasped the basics of cryptocurrency and are ready to explore more sophisticated investment strategies. Here, we'll delve into risk management techniques, the potential of staking and yield farming for earning passive income, and the intricacies of leveraging and margin trading. These concepts, while more complex, can significantly enhance your ability to grow your crypto holdings and manage risks effectively.

CHAPTER 6

RISK MANAGEMENT

Risk management is crucial in cryptocurrency investing due to the market's inherent volatility. Here we cover strategies to protect your investments and maintain a healthy portfolio.

Setting Stop Losses and Taking Profits

Stop Losses: A stop loss is an order to sell a security when it reaches a certain price, helping limit your losses. In crypto trading, setting a stop loss can protect you from significant downturns in a volatile market.

Taking Profits: While holding for long-term gains can be beneficial, it's also important to take profits at strategic times. Setting targets for taking profits can ensure you capitalize on price surges without being caught in a subsequent downturn.

Managing Your Investment Portfolio

Diversification is key in managing a crypto investment portfolio. It's wise not to put all your capital into one asset. Spread your investments across different cryptocurrencies, sectors (like DeFi, NFTs, or utility tokens), and even investment types (like staking, trading, or ICOs).

Rebalancing your portfolio periodically to maintain your desired asset allocation can help manage risk and take advantage of market movements.

Psychological Aspects of Trading and Investing

The psychological element of investing, often called investor psychology, plays a significant role in decision-making. Fear of missing out (FOMO) can lead to buying at peaks, while panic selling during downturns can result in losses. Cultivate a disciplined approach, sticking to your investment strategy regardless of market noise.

CHAPTER 7

STAKING AND YIELD FARMING

Staking and yield farming offer avenues to earn passive income through your cryptocurrency holdings.

Earning Passive Income through Cryptocurrency

Staking: Many cryptocurrencies allow you to earn rewards by staking your holdings in a wallet to support the network's operations, such as transaction validation on a proof-of-stake (PoS) blockchain.

Yield Farming: In the DeFi space, yield farming involves lending your crypto assets to others through smart contracts to earn interest or other rewards. It's more complex and risky than staking but can offer higher returns.

Understanding DeFi (Decentralized Finance)

DeFi represents a shift from traditional, centralized financial systems to peer-to-peer finance enabled by decentralized technologies built on blockchain. DeFi platforms allow users to lend, borrow, trade, and earn interest on their crypto assets without the need for traditional banks or financial intermediaries.

Risks and Rewards of Staking and Yield Farming

While staking and yield farming can provide attractive returns, they come with their own sets of risks. These include smart contract vulnerabilities, impermanent loss in liquidity pools, and the volatility of rewards. Thorough research and risk assessment are essential before engaging in these activities.

CHAPTER 8

LEVERAGING AND MARGIN TRADING

Leverage and margin trading amplify your trading power but also increase risk.

How to Use Leverage Wisely

Leverage allows traders to borrow money to increase their trading position beyond what would be possible with their own capital alone. While this can magnify gains, it also increases the potential for losses.

Using leverage wisely involves understanding the terms of the leverage, carefully managing the size of leveraged positions, and employing strict risk management practices.

Risks Associated with Margin Trading

Margin trading involves borrowing funds to trade cryptocurrencies, increasing your buying power but also your potential losses. The risks include the possibility of a margin call if your account value falls below a certain level, requiring you to deposit more funds or sell your assets at a loss.

Best Practices for Margin Trading

Successful margin traders use strategies such as setting stop-loss orders to limit potential losses, carefully selecting entry and exit points, and never investing more than they can afford to lose. Continuous learning and staying informed about market conditions are also crucial.

By mastering these advanced investment techniques, you can enhance your ability to navigate the cryptocurrency market more effectively. However, always remember that with higher potential returns comes increased risk. Diligent research, ongoing education, and a disciplined approach to risk management are essential for success in the volatile world of cryptocurrency investing.

PART III
BEYOND TRADING

Cryptocurrency trading is just the tip of the iceberg when it comes to the transformative power of blockchain technology. This section will guide you through the broader implications of blockchain, its applications beyond cryptocurrencies, the regulatory landscape, security measures, and the significance of community within the crypto space. Designed for absolute beginners, this comprehensive exploration will help you understand the vast potential and the practical considerations of engaging with blockchain and cryptocurrency on a deeper level.

CHAPTER 9

BLOCKCHAIN AND ITS APPLICATIONS

Beyond Cryptocurrency: The Power of Blockchain

Blockchain technology is the backbone of cryptocurrency, but its applications extend far beyond just enabling digital currencies. At its core, a blockchain is a decentralized ledger of transactions, immutable and transparent, making it secure by design. This foundational technology has the potential to revolutionize industries by providing a new way to process and record transactions without the need for a central authority.

NFTs (Non-Fungible Tokens) and Their Economic Impact

Non-Fungible Tokens (NFTs) have emerged as a groundbreaking application of blockchain technology, allowing digital assets to be uniquely owned and traded. Unlike cryptocurrencies, which are interchangeable, each NFT is distinct, representing ownership of a specific digital item, such as artwork, music, or collectibles. The rise of NFTs has transformed the art world and content creation, enabling artists and creators to monetize their digital works directly and securely through blockchain.

The Future of Blockchain in Various Industries

The potential of blockchain extends into numerous sectors, including finance, healthcare, supply chain management, and more. In finance, blockchain can streamline payments, reduce fraud, and improve access to financial services. Healthcare can benefit from secure, interoperable patient records. Supply chains can become more transparent and efficient, with every step of a product's journey verifiable on the blockchain. As technology evolves, its adoption across these and other industries is expected to grow, offering opportunities for innovation and improvement.

CHAPTER 10

REGULATION AND SECURITY

Keeping Your Investments Safe (Security Practices, Wallets, Exchanges)

As you venture deeper into the world of cryptocurrency, prioritizing security is paramount. Implementing robust security practices, choosing secure wallets, and using reputable exchanges can protect your investments from theft and hacking. Hardware wallets offer enhanced security for storing cryptocurrencies offline, while two-factor authentication and using strong, unique passwords are essential practices for online accounts.

Understanding Regulatory Changes and Their Impact

The regulatory environment for cryptocurrency is rapidly evolving as governments around the world seek to address the challenges and opportunities presented by digital currencies.

Staying informed about regulatory changes in your jurisdiction is crucial, as these can impact the legality, taxation, and over-all landscape of cryptocurrency investing and usage.

Avoiding Scams and Ponzi Schemes

The cryptocurrency space, while offering numerous opportunities, is also rife with scams and fraudulent schemes. Educating yourself on common types of scams, such as phishing, fake ICOs, and Ponzi schemes, is essential to safeguard your investments. Always conduct thorough research before investing in any project and be wary of offers that seem too good to be true.

CHAPTER 11

BUILDING A CRYPTO COMMUNITY

Importance of Community in Crypto Investing

The cryptocurrency community is a vital resource for investors, offering support, knowledge, and insights. Engaging with the community can enhance your understanding of the market, provide access to new opportunities, and offer a sense of belonging in the rapidly evolving crypto space.

Leveraging Social Media and Forums for Insights

Social media platforms and online forums are hubs for cryptocurrency enthusiasts and investors. Platforms like Twitter, Reddit, and specialized crypto forums host vibrant discussions, analysis, and news sharing. Participating in these communities can keep you informed about market trends, project developments, and investment strategies.

Networking and Collaboration Opportunities

Building relationships within the crypto community can open doors to collaboration and networking opportunities. Whether you're interested in developing blockchain projects, exploring investment opportunities, or simply learning more about the technology, connecting with like-minded individuals can enrich your crypto journey.

As you delve into the broader implications and applications of blockchain technology, remember that the field is constantly evolving. Staying informed, prioritizing security, and engaging with the community are key to navigating the complexities of the crypto world. The journey beyond trading into the realms of blockchain's transformative potential is an exciting and rewarding path, offering endless opportunities for learning, investment, and innovation.

PART IV
PLANNING FOR THE FUTURE

Navigating the world of cryptocurrency can be exhilarating and, at times, overwhelming. However, as you become more familiar with this digital landscape, it's essential to consider how it fits into your broader financial picture. This section will guide you through integrating cryptocurrency into your overall financial plan, including retirement and estate planning. We'll also explore the future of cryptocurrency investing, touching on emerging trends and technologies, global adoption, and predictions for the coming decade.

CHAPTER 12

CRYPTOCURRENCY AS PART OF YOUR OVERALL FINANCIAL PLAN

Integrating Crypto with Traditional Financial Planning

Cryptocurrency can be a valuable addition to your investment portfolio, offering diversification beyond traditional stocks, bonds, and real estate. However, due to its volatility, it's crucial to balance your crypto investments with more stable assets. A financial advisor familiar with digital currencies can help you determine an appropriate allocation based on your risk tolerance and financial goals.

Retirement Planning with Cryptocurrency

Considering cryptocurrency in your retirement planning may offer growth potential that traditional retirement accounts lack. Some platforms and services now allow for the inclusion of cryptocurrencies in Individual Retirement Accounts (IRAs) and other pension plans. However, remember the risks and consider maintaining a diversified portfolio.

Estate Planning and Passing on Crypto Assets

Estate planning for cryptocurrency is essential to ensure your digital assets are passed on according to your wishes. Unlike traditional assets, cryptocurrencies require specific information to access (e.g., private keys, wallet passwords). Include detailed instructions in your estate plan and consider using a digital asset management service to simplify the process for your heirs.

CHAPTER 13

THE FUTURE OF CRYPTOCURRENCY INVESTING

Emerging Trends and Technologies (AI, Quantum Computing)

The intersection of cryptocurrency with emerging technologies like Artificial Intelligence (AI) and quantum computing holds promising potential. AI can enhance market analysis, predict trends, and improve security, while quantum computing poses both challenges and opportunities for cryptographic security. Staying informed about these developments will be crucial for future investors.

Global Adoption and Its Economic Implications

Cryptocurrency's journey towards global adoption is progressing, with businesses, governments, and financial institutions increasingly recognizing and integrating digital currencies. This trend towards mainstream acceptance could lead to significant economic implications, including increased financial inclusivity and a shift in how we think about money and transactions.

Predictions for the Next Decade

Predicting the future of cryptocurrency is challenging due to its rapidly evolving nature. However, several trends are likely to shape its trajectory:

- Increased regulatory clarity could lead to more stable markets and broader adoption.
- The growth of decentralized finance (DeFi) may challenge traditional financial systems.
- Innovations in blockchain technology could lead to more efficient, secure, and scalable networks.

The evolution of cryptocurrency and blockchain technology offers a wealth of opportunities for those prepared to adapt and innovate. As we look to the future, the potential for digital currencies to transform our financial system and society is vast. However, as with any investment, it's essential to proceed with caution, stay informed, and make decisions that align with your overall financial strategy.

In this comprehensive guide, we've explored the essentials of cryptocurrency investing, from the basics to advanced strategies and the broader implications of blockchain technology.

Whether you're a beginner or looking to deepen your understanding, remember that the key to success in this dynamic
field is continuous learning and adaptability. As you plan for
the future, consider how cryptocurrency fits into your financial landscape and stay abreast of the latest trends and developments. The world of cryptocurrency is ever-evolving,
and the possibilities are as limitless as your willingness to
explore them.

CONCLUSION
TAKING CONTROL OF YOUR FINANCIAL FUTURE WITH CRYPTOCURRENCY

Embarking on the journey of cryptocurrency investment is a bold step towards taking control of your financial future. This guide has navigated you through the essential landscapes of cryptocurrency, from the basics to more advanced investment strategies and the implications of blockchain technology in various sectors. As we conclude, let's recap the key strategies that will help solidify your success in the crypto world, provide encouragement for continuous growth, and outline the next steps to make your first or next investment more informed and strategic.

Recapping Key Strategies for Success

Educate Yourself Continuously: The world of cryptocurrency is fast-evolving, making continuous learning crucial. Stay updated with the latest trends, technologies, and market dynamics.

Start Small and Diversify: Begin your investment journey with amounts you're comfortable losing and diversify your portfolio to spread risk.

Use Reliable Sources and Tools: Engage with reputable news outlets, use secure wallets, and trade on trusted exchanges.

Implement Risk Management: Apply strategies such as setting stop-loss orders and taking profits at predetermined levels to protect your investments.

Plan for the Long Term: Consider how cryptocurrency fits into your overall financial plan, including retirement and estate planning.

Encouragement to Continue Learning and Adapting

The path to becoming a successful crypto investor is paved with challenges and learning opportunities. Embrace both as they come. The crypto community is vast and supportive, offering countless resources for education and growth. Remember, every expert was once a beginner. Your willingness to learn, adapt, and stay informed will be your greatest assets in navigating the cryptocurrency market.

Next Steps: Making Your First Investment

If you're ready to make your first investment or looking to refine your strategy, here's a step-by-step approach to get started on the right foot:

1. **Set Clear Goals**: Define what you want to achieve with your crypto investments.
2. **Research**: Delve into the projects or coins you're interested in. Understand their value proposition, technology, and market position.
3. **Choose a Secure Wallet**: Select a wallet that fits your needs and ensures the security of your assets.
4. **Select a Reputable Exchange**: Sign up with an exchange that offers the assets you're interested in and is known for its security and customer service.
5. **Start Small**: Make your first investment modest to gain experience with less risk.
6. **Monitor and Adjust**: Keep an eye on your investments and the market, ready to adjust your strategy as needed.

APPENDICES

Glossary of Terms

- **Blockchain**: A distributed ledger technology that records transactions across many computers securely and transparently.
- **Cryptocurrency**: Digital or virtual currency that uses cryptography for security and operates independently of a central bank.
- **Wallet**: A digital tool that allows you to store, send, and receive cryptocurrencies.
- **Exchange**: A platform where you can buy, sell, and trade cryptocurrencies.
- **ICO (Initial Coin Offering)**: A fundraising method where new projects sell their underlying crypto tokens in exchange for bitcoin and ether.

Recommended Reading and Resources

- **"The Bitcoin Standard" by Saifedean Ammous**: A comprehensive look into the historical context and economic properties of Bitcoin.
- **CoinMarketCap**: A website for tracking the capitalization of various cryptocurrencies.
- **Crypto Subreddits and Forums**: Online communities like r/CryptoCurrency and BitcoinTalk for discussions and advice.

- **How do I buy cryptocurrency?** Start by creating an account on a cryptocurrency exchange, then deposit fiat money, and purchase the cryptocurrency of your choice.

- **Is cryptocurrency safe?** While cryptocurrency technologies offer secure transactions, the market is volatile, and there are risks from hacking. Proper security measures and due diligence are essential.

- **Can I lose all my money in cryptocurrency?** Yes, due to the market's volatility, it's possible to experience significant losses. Invest only what you can afford to lose and implement risk management strategies.

LEAVE A REVIEW – LET OTHER READERS KNOW WHAT YOU THINK

Please share your thoughts on this book with others by leaving a review on the site that you bought it from. If you purchased the book from Amazon, please leave us an honest review on this book's Amazon page. This is vital so that other potential readers can see and use your unbiased opinion to make purchasing decisions, we can understand what our customers think about our products, and our author can see your. It will only take a few minutes of your time, but is valuable to other potential customers, our authors. Thank you!